Mr. McDoogle's Yellow Submarine

Written and Illustrated By:

Marie Whitton

For My Husband
Greg

For My Children
Gregory, Ann-Marie &
Kimberly

For My
Grandchildren

Fishing

BOATS

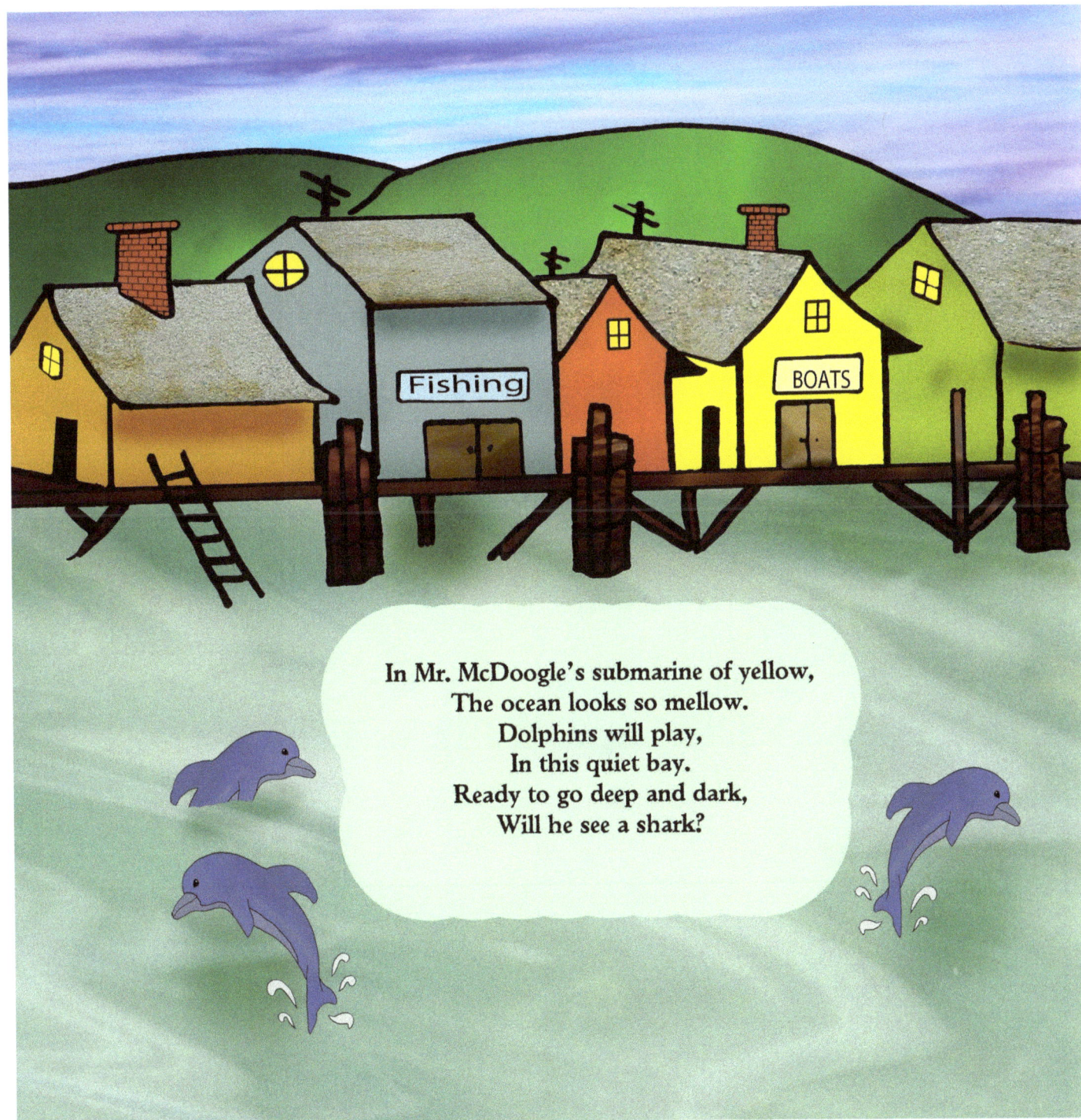

In Mr. McDoogle's submarine of yellow,
The ocean looks so mellow.
Dolphins will play,
In this quiet bay.
Ready to go deep and dark,
Will he see a shark?

Are there any secrets in this ocean?
It does have a lot of motion.
Mr. McDoogle wants to learn it's history,
So, he will have to dive to find it's mystery.

Not very deep - the water is crystal clear,
Quiet and peaceful - no sounds to hear.
Mr. McDoogle will see all sorts of unusual sights,
The water is still letting in the sun's light.

Mr. McDoogle can see fish of red - yellow and blue,
There is a ship wreck - It is not new.

Sponges and corral are lots,
Scattered over the ocean bottom like little dots.

Lobsters are on the move traveling far,
They had to go around a sand bar.
Watching this parade was a sting ray,
This is great - Mr. McDoogle did say.

Mr. McDoogle goes -
darker and deeper,
He is a true peeper.

Mr. McDoogle is seeing whales,
sharks and squid,
All from the top - they were hid.

There are secrets to search for,
Have to go deeper looking for more.

To the bottom - It is getting cold,
Mr. McDoogle was very bold.

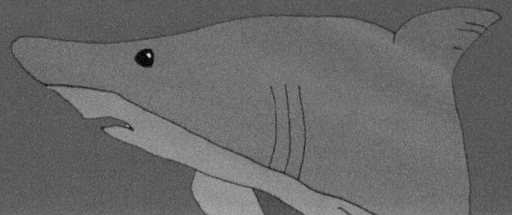

Mr. McDoogle's eye was caught by a
wonderful vision,
Had to take a closer look that was his mission.
Is that a volcano he was seeing?
Shining lots of light and nothing was fleeing.

Lava was dancing and flowing from the top,
The volcano looked like it was about to pop.

The water turned to warm,
Unusual creatures - was the norm.

It's time to leave this secret place,
For another day - Mr. McDoogle will
return to this space.
In his submarine of yellow,
The ocean was not so mellow.